The Buildings of Windsor

720
942

MOR

Hertfordshire
COUNTY COUNCIL
Community Information

10 SEP 2003

10/12

2 8 JUN 2001

1 1 ... 2003

1 ... 2003

L32a

Please renew/return this item by the last date shown.

So that your telephone call is charged at local rate, please call the numbers as set out below:

	From Area codes 01923 or 0208:	From the rest of Herts:
Renewals:	01923 471373	01438 737373
Enquiries:	01923 471333	01438 737333
Minicom:	01923 471599	01438 737599

L32b

720.942

1 The Norman Gateway, the entrance from the Middle Ward to the Upper, is really the Inner Gateway. There has probably been a gate at this point for centuries and parts of the present masonry date to a rebuild of the 1360s. Most of its present appearance is due to Wyattville nearly five centuries later; he completely rebuilt the left-hand tower.

The Buildings
of Windsor

RICHARD K. MORRISS

With photographs by Ken Hoverd

ALAN SUTTON PUBLISHING LIMITED

First published in the United Kingdom in 1994
Alan Sutton Publishing Limited
Phoenix Mill · Far Thrupp · Stroud · Gloucestershire

First published in the United States of America in 1994
Alan Sutton Publishing Inc · 83 Washington Street · Dover
NH 03820

British Library Cataloguing in Publication Data

A catalogue record for this book is available from the British
Library.

ISBN 0-7509-0562-X

Library of Congress Cataloging in Publication Data applied for

Cover illustations: front: *the ancient Clewer Tower of Windsor
Castle*; inset: *Market Cross House*; back: *Church Street*.

Typeset in 11/14 Times.
Typesetting and origination by
Alan Sutton Publishing Limited.
Printed in Great Britain by
Ebenezer Baylis, Worcester.

Contents

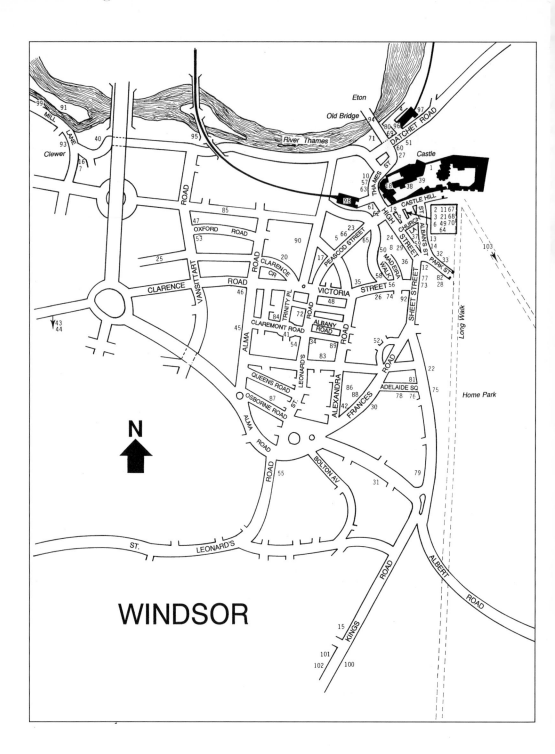

Introduction

About a mile off Windsor Castle appeares standing on a hill . . .
with walls and battlements round. [It] is the finest pallace the
king has . . . it is a pretty great ascent to the town, which is
well built – something suitable to London by reason of its
affinity to the Court.

(Celia Fiennes c. 1680s)

Historic Windsor, home of the British monarchy and once the
effective centre of Empire, is one of the major tourist
attractions in the world – though it is to the castle, rather than
to the town, that the visitors are mainly drawn. The castle is,
indeed, the only reason for the town's existence, and there was
little on this spot until it was built. The meaning of its name is
lost in time, but Windsor is generally thought to mean 'the
place where there was a windlass on the river bank'. Perhaps
this was for hauling boats up a shallow reach of the Thames in
low water, or perhaps a place where boats were unloaded – but
the place where that historic windlass may have been was not
the site of present-day Windsor. The town copied the name
from a much older settlement a few miles downstream, known
today as Old Windsor.

Recent archaeological work has shown Old Windsor to have
been an important Saxon site, the Thames at one time being the
border between the powerful kingdoms of Mercia, to the north,
and Sussex, to the south. Windlesora became the site of a royal
palace used, among others, by Edward the Confessor. This was
a base from which to enjoy the royal Saxons' passion for
hunting – in what was to become the Great Park. The
conquering Normans shared the Saxons' love of the hunt but
were also concerned to keep their new and rather unwilling
subjects under control. They did this mainly by using a new

Perched on top of a chalk outcrop, Windsor Castle has dominated this part of the Thames valley for over nine hundred years, ever since William the Conqueror chose this site for one of the key fortresses to protect London and the important river valley route to it.

type of fortification – the motte-and-bailey castle – and chose suitable sites all over the country. In the strategically important Thames valley there was only one good defensive site between London and Wallingford, a chalk cliff at the extreme north-west corner of Old Windsor parish, straddling the boundary with the neighbouring parish of Clewer and on the very edge of Berkshire. This bluff commanded the western approach to the capital, was conveniently a day's march away from it, was on the banks of the navigable Thames and was only a few miles from the palace in Old Windsor – and the hunting.

Clewer had belonged to King Harold before the Conquest and afterwards was given to Ralph, son of Seifride. In about 1070 a half a hide of the manor, which included much of the hill overlooking the river, was taken back by William for a rental of 12*s* (60p) a year and a new castle was built on top of the cliff. Until 1107 the Court still met at the old palace but

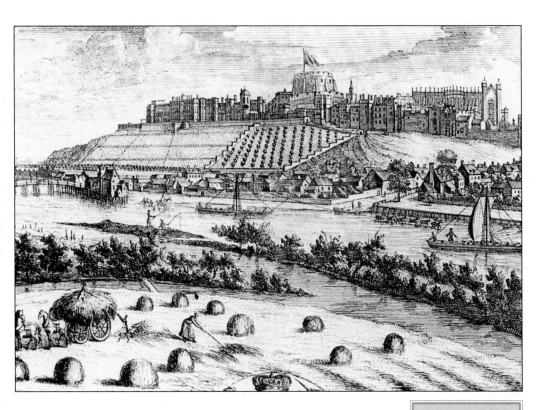

John Kip was one of the best and most prolific of early eighteenth-century illustrators. His view of Windsor from the opposite bank of the Thames was probably drawn in the early 1720s and shows the medieval castle dominating the town. The busy river traffic, the old timber bridge, and the haymaking in the foreground add to the scene.

Henry I built a new one within the new castle. The Court met officially at what was now called New Windsor for the first time in 1110. After that, Old Windsor declined while a new town developed outside the gates of the new castle.

New Windsor remained a fairly small town – of fewer than a thousand inhabitants or so – right up until Tudor times. Nevertheless, throughout the past nine hundred years the town's importance in history has been out of all proportion to its size. It was the great Assize of Windsor that led to the introduction of trial by jury instead of trial by combat, and from Windsor in the summer of 1215 King John rode to nearby Runnymede and reluctantly signed Magna Carta, that great symbol of the English constitution. Throughout its existence, the town's fortunes have been closely linked to the monarchy, and to the extent that individual monarchs did, or did not, enjoy living in the castle. Surprisingly, the town seldom

suffered because of the political goings on within those high grey embattled walls. The castle was only laid to siege twice in its history, both times being held by supporters of King John.

The age-old ties between town and crown were symbolized during the First World War when anti-German feeling ran high. The royal family name, Saxe-Coburg, was considered somewhat unpatriotic – especially given the close relations that they had with the German Kaiser and his family. On 17 July 1917 King George changed the family name, creating the House of Windsor – still, of course, on the throne, and still frequent visitors to the castle.

Although the new castle dominated the small town, it also depended on it. The castle needed a good supply of food, goods, craftsmen and labourers. For this reason people were encouraged to come and live and trade in the new town,

2 Being central to the affairs of state for over a thousand years, it is not surprising that Windsor has been home to many of the rich, the powerful and the famous. This fine mid-seventeenth-century house in Church Street is said to have been the home of Nell Gwynn, the Hereford-born mistress of Charles II. She probably lived in Burford House nearby and was just one of his several mistresses. The narrow timber-framed 'wings' of this symmetrical composition are most unusual.

although its earliest known charter, given by Edward I, only dates back to 1277. The medieval core of New Windsor was just outside the main castle gate, with houses around a roughly triangular market place between the gate and the new parish church of St John, first mentioned in the early twelfth century. This once-large market place has since been infilled by buildings, as the temporary stalls became less and less temporary, and eventually became replaced by permanent houses. This process of 'market infilling' can be seen in many other medieval towns and usually results in the same type of narrow, picturesque streets. In Windsor they cover the area between the castle, parish church and Guild-hall, and include Church Lane, Church Street, Market Street and Queen Charlotte Street – at just 51 ft 10 in long claimed to be the shortest street in England. Until quite recently, Market Street was called Butcher Row, Church Street was known as Fish Street – giving some indication of what merchandise was sold where – and Castle Hill used to be called King's Market Place.

By the thirteenth century the town had spread out along the three main roads leading out from the centre. Thames Street (formerly Bishop's Street) curved its way down past the castle to a bridge over the river that may have replaced a ford as early as 1172. The river bank at this point had been marshy and empty before the arrival of the Normans, but they set about reclaiming the bank, and building wharfs and warehouses as New Windsor became an important port on the river – then the principal transport artery of southern England. Park Street (once Pound Street) continued the line of the High Street to the south-east and was the main road to London by way of Old Windsor and Staines. The unusually named Peascod Street, leading towards Clewer Fields, is a reminder of the importance of the humble pea in the medieval diet. The houses tended to straggle along the line of these streets. There were still large areas of fields between and, well away from the main town, were the separate settlements of Clewer and Dedworth. Little changed from this basic plan until the start of the nineteenth century.

Across the river was Eton, which grew up on either side of the road leading from Windsor Bridge to Slough. Such bridgehead settlements on the opposite banks from the

principal town are common – but Eton's relationship with
Windsor is unusual. It was in existence long before New
Windsor and was, and still is, in a different county –
Buckinghamshire. It was, and still is, independent of its larger
neighbour and in the medieval period had its own market, fair
and, of course, its famous college. The school, incidentally,
was set up in Eton by a Lancastrian king, Henry VI; a Yorkist
king, Edward IV, then tried to emulate its chapel inside
Windsor Castle – a typical example of the former rivalry
between the two towns. Despite its comparatively small size,
Eton is still very much a town in its own right – a fact probably
made more obvious since the old Windsor Bridge was
pedestrianized in recent years and traffic diverted to the new
bridge upstream, opened in 1966.

New Windsor, like most medieval towns in England,
suffered badly from the effects of the Black Death in 1348

4 In recent years Windsor has become an important base for many national and international companies and many new buildings are being erected for office accommodation. Close by the Riverside station is Riverside House, a brand new complex mimicking the Tudor Gothic elements of the castle. At least, architecturally, it is a bit of fun, and it does respect the Gothic of William Tite's station buildings.

5 Windsor is a popular shopping centre for this part of the Thames valley, a fact reflected in several new developments, such as this one, King Edward's Court, opened in 1980. It is the typically bland and regionless pseudo-Vernacular type – found anywhere in England.

6 The Three Tuns, on the corner of Church Lane and Market Street, is, despite appearances, a timber-framed building. It was put up in about 1515, originally as the Guild-hall of the Guild of the Holy Trinity. It was jettied on both street fronts – and the original beams and the diagonal 'dragon' beam can still be seen in the ceiling of the ground floor rooms. The building was clearly remodelled in the eighteenth and nineteenth centuries.

10 Although an often controversial character in his long period as Prince of Wales, Edward VII proved to be a popular monarch. His bust sits in the Olde King and Castle on Thames Street, built, oddly, in 1917 – at the height of the First World War.

9 A statue of Prince Frederick of Denmark, Queen Anne's husband, in the east end of the town hall.

11 Windsor has been aware of its tourist potential for many years and, in the older part of the town at least, great efforts have been made to improve the quality of the townscape. Church Street is typical in being both pedestrianized and well paved with setts. Their rich texture is so much better than the bland monotony of tarmac or asphalt.

Charles himself was imprisoned for a while at Windsor in December 1648 – his arrival causing a riot in the town between supporters of the two sides. He left Windsor for his trial in Westminster – and his body was brought back for burial after his execution.

The town had suffered from the pressures put upon it during the war, trying to cope with being a garrison town, and during the Commonwealth suffered even more. The castle was no longer the home of royalty and of the court, so there was no need for the service industries that had largely kept the town going. The return of Charles II in 1660 was more than welcome and led to another revival in Windsor's fortunes,

especially as the king saw it as one of his favourite homes, and set about rebuilding the castle and landscaping the Great Park. The members of the Court were frequently at the castle and several courtiers built houses in the town. The Guild-hall was rebuilt again in this short-lived period of prosperity.

When Charles's brother, James II, took the throne, in 1685, the political ramifications of his Catholicism were enormous and resulted in the arrival in England of William of Orange three years later. Progressing through the west of England and meeting no opposition, Prince William arrived and took Windsor Castle and summoned peers of the realm to him. During these discussions it became clear that James had no future as king and would be deposed – but he then fled, at the second attempt, to the Continent, and William and Mary, James's daughter, took the throne. For the next hundred years,

12 While Windsor became an important place for the aristocracy to own or rent houses, it never quite made it as a fashionable resort for the middle and upper classes – despite the construction of several quite grand terraces in the later Georgian period. This stuccoed early nineteenth-century example on Park Street was clearly influenced by the work of Regency architects such as Nash.

13 This part of the Royal Mews, on St Alban's Street, now houses an exhibition of the queen's carriages – and some of her many presents. The fairly plain brick range with its large double doors was designed by Blore. To all intents and purposes a part of the life of the castle, the mews are outside its walls and in the town.

14 Beyond Edward Blore's castellated gatehouse to the Royal Riding School off St Alban's Street is the late-seventeenth-century Burford House, encased in yet more of Blore's heavy-handed work. The riding school and adjacent mews were finished in 1842. The name of the street is derived from Nell's first son by Charles II, who was created Earl of St Albans.

Windsor was to see little of royalty, apart from poor Queen Anne, and the town stagnated.

Only when George III decided to take an interest in the castle in the last two decades of the eighteenth century did the town grow again, and continued to do so erratically under the patronage of successive monarchs – George IV, William IV, and Queen Victoria. In 1775 the town had around 4,000 inhabitants which, despite a slight decline at the turn of the century, had risen to almost 6,000 by the 1830s and to over 10,000 by the end of Victoria's long reign. The influence of Victoria and, for a tragically much shorter period, her consort, Prince Albert, have left their mark on the town. At the start of her reign the physical health of the townspeople was under constant threat from poor drainage. A report of 1842 on sanitary conditions stated that the facilities in Windsor, because of 'the continuity of the palace, the wealth of the inhabitants, and the situation, might have been expected to be superior in this respect to any other provincial town'. The opposite was true, and the exasperated inspector added that 'of all the towns visited by me, Windsor is the worst beyond all comparison'. Thanks in no small way to the direct and indirect pressures of the young royal couple, matters materially improved throughout the next few decades. Since the middle of Victoria's reign, the irresistible spread of London's suburbs, coupled with the improvements in transport from the mid-nineteenth century onwards, has made the royal borough attractive to commuters.

Fortunately, Windsor retains the unique character given by its castle and its ties with the monarchy – although that character is certainly not helped by the intrusive roar of planes heading in and out of nearby Heathrow all day long. It has to cope with the immense pressures put on it as the nation's major tourist attraction – an estimated three million visitors arriving each year. It is still a garrison town, but since the end of the eighteenth century most of the soldiers not billeted inside the castle have been accommodated in purpose-built barracks rather than foisted on often-unwilling local householders. Industry has never really been a significant factor in its prosperity, but in recent years there has been a growth in the amount of office accommodation with several major companies basing their headquarters or regional offices in the town.

One less-than-welcome event in its recent history came as part of the ill-judged boundary reshufflings of the early 1970s. As a result, the town's historic independence ended. On the first day of 1974 the administration of Windsor was amalgamated with that of Maidenhead – a town with its own traditions and history, and the town chosen as the location of the new headquarters for the combined district council. Twenty years on and the boundaries all over the country are again being interfered with; perhaps this time Windsor's historic status will be restored.

The doorcases of the terraces of Adelaide Square, built in the very early years of Victoria's reign, are all of the same basic pattern, with quarter-round fluted pilasters and plain fanlights.

The mid-eighteenth-century doorcase of 5 Park Street – Ann Foorde's House – with a 'broken pediment' supported on fluted Doric columns.

A late eighteenth-century doorcase, of 24 Park Street, with rather odd brick surround and a distinctive fanlight.

Detail of the door canopy of Nell Gwynn's House, 6 Church Street – a mid-seventeenth-century town house combining brick construction with timber framing.

Architectural Character

As with most aspects of this royal borough, its architectural character is largely dominated by the battlemented bulk of the castle. The town seems to keep a respectful distance from its walls, leaving a green sward between Thames Street and the defences. As with most of the present appearance of the castle, this is only a nineteenth-century 'improvement'. This area was almost certainly clear of buildings when the castle was built, to deprive any potential aggressor of cover and also to leave room for a deep, defensive ditch. Over the years the ditch was infilled, buildings were built up against the outside of the walls and, by the end of the seventeenth century, lined the castle side of the street.

Only when Wyatt began remodelling the castle at the start of the nineteenth century did the Crown begin buying up these houses and demolishing them – finishing the process early in the 1850s. During the same period, other improvements designed to increase the privacy of those in the castle included the closure of several old roads and paths, and the creation of new ones. For example, Park Street, once the start of the route from the town to London via Old Windsor, was blocked at the edge of the Home Park in 1851 and traffic diverted to a new road – Albert Road.

Outside the gates, the layout of the town reflects its historic growth – the tightly knit streets of the medieval core, the older buildings lining the main streets leading from it, the various much more rigidly planned nineteenth-century developments infilling the remaining open spaces and the modern estates on the edges. In the centre there is a greater mix of buildings, because development has always been piecemeal and little dramatic happened for centuries. Also, in the typical English way of things, the rich lived cheek-by-jowl with the poor. This meant that large mansions and town houses were built close to much humbler dwellings – a legacy still evident in the town. In the burgeoning new suburbs of the nineteenth century, planning had become much more class conscious, so the spacious semi-detached houses around Holy Trinity or Clarence Crescent were a world away from the rigid lines of artisan terraces elsewhere.

Most buildings in the town give the appearance of being built of brick, stone being largely confined to the castle and the churches, and timber framing virtually non-existent. As with most historic towns, this initial impression is quite misleading. It is true that there are few stone buildings in the town. The reason for this is quite simple – the local stone is a very poor material for building. Chalk is simply not weather-proof enough and while it could be, and was, used extensively for corework inside the walls of the castle, its use elsewhere was virtually non-existent. It could be used in conjunction with flint – a native form of silica often found in association with chalk deposits but usually only found as small rounded pebbles a few inches in diameter. When used for building, flints were generally roughly coursed in a thick mortar. The flints on the outer faces were usually split, or 'knapped', to give a flat surface designed to improve their appearance and texture. The only important building left made of flint is the Norman parish church of St Andrew, in Clewer.

Chalk was clearly totally unsuitable for the outer skins of the walls of the castle, but the monarchs who built it could afford to import stone from other areas both by water, on the Thames, or even overland and often from hundreds of miles away. Only when transport improved dramatically in the nineteenth century could most other buildings of pretension be constructed of imported stone – churches and banks in particular.

Until the late seventeenth century Windsor was a timber-framed town, and many buildings in the town are still timber framed, despite all appearances to the contrary. Timber was a cheap material and easy to obtain. The original castle had been defended by timber palisades and contained timber-framed buildings. The felled trees were usually measured and sawn in

16 The widespread acceptance of brick as a fashionable building material from, the late seventeenth century onwards led to different ways of 'up grading' houses. The front of The Limes, Mill Lane, Clewer, is of late seventeenth-century brick built onto the front of an otherwise timber-framed structure.

16 This rear wing of The Limes shows its true character. The brick nogging in this case is a later modification and the original panel size may suggest that this could date to the early sixteenth century or even a little before.

17 Perhaps the most obvious example of timber framing in Windsor is this building, 86–7 Peascod Street. Although claimed to date to the fifteenth-century, the surviving framework would suggest a much later date – possibly around 1600. Even then, all of the front 'frame' is the result of a restoration of 1976.

18 The fabric of the Horseshoe Cloister may have been radically restored – and effectively rebuilt – by Gilbert Scott in 1871, but the original design was copied faithfully. Begun in 1478, the ranges are of timber framing, but the panel infills were of brick – brick nogging – and a very early example of this type of hybrid construction.

the carpenter's yard. They would be temporarily slotted together into individual frames on the floor, and usually each mortise and tenon joint would be marked by a type of Roman numeral gouged or cut into the face of the timber. These 'carpenters' marks' were designed to make sure that, after the frames had been dismantled and carted to site, they could be re-erected in the right order. The joints themselves were generally strengthened by round dowels, called pegs. Carpenters' marks can sometimes be seen – and pegs almost certainly can – on surviving timber frames and can give a good

19 This row of houses flanking the east side of the High Street is essentially timber framed – simply encased with brick or lath and plaster in the eighteenth century to bring them more up to date and they were rewindowed in the process. To the right is Queen Charlotte Street, said to be the shortest street in England.

20 The area around Holy Trinity Church was developed in the first half of the nineteenth century for the middle classes and, in particular, to provide houses for army officers. These grand houses in Clarence Crescent were probably built in the early years of Victoria's reign. At this time, brick was seen as out of fashion, so the houses were stuccoed. Note how even the two apparently detached houses to the left are actually semi-detached.

21 Church Street has a good collection of large seventeenth-century brick town houses. No. 4 has seven bays with the centre one projecting. The sashes are later – the glazing bars are too thin to be early. The brick bond, alternating courses of end-bricks – 'headers' – and of bricks laid lengthways – 'stretchers' – is called an English Bond.

idea whether the work is real or not. The spaces between the timbers had to be infilled of course – usually by wattle and daub.

Windsor only has a handful of obviously timber-framed buildings – the best being a rear wing of The Limes in Clewer which could date from the sixteenth century or earlier. An apparently more complete timber frame is 86–7 Peascod Street, said to date from the early fifteenth century. The construction of the end frames would suggest that it is much later – possibly being built in the seventeenth century. The front is virtually all new, having been radically restored in 1976.

Most of the other timber frames in Windsor have been

22 This long but relatively plain stock-brick terrace on the King's Road manages to impress by its size and uniformity. Built around 1800, most of the original glazing and doors have been retained. More surprisingly, the railings around the little basement yards – or 'areas' – remain. Most of the cast-iron balconies survive, too, and their railings have a slightly Gothic feel about them.

hidden for aesthetic reasons. Architecture has its fickle changes of taste, just as any other art form, and with the increasing popularity of brick and classical simplicity from the end of the seventeenth century onwards, timber frames were seen as positively antediluvian and had to be demolished or disguised. Those who could not afford a completely new brick building added just a brick front; those not able even to do that plastered over the framing and pretended that their building was made of brick – but had been plastered. Only round the back of such buildings, or sometimes within, is the real story told – and many of the buildings in the town are well worth a closer inspection.

Although brick had been introduced to Britain by the Romans, it was virtually ignored for a thousand years after they left – despite being well known as a building material in

Europe. The revival of brick in Britain during the late medieval period was felt early on in this part of the Thames valley – some two and a half million bricks being made at Slough for the buildings of Eton College in the mid-fifteenth century for example. Over the Thames in Windsor its use was less dramatic – but the eighteen thousand-odd bricks used in the panel infills of the otherwise timber-framed Horseshoe Cloister next to St George's Chapel are a rare early example of this technique. Usually brick infills – or nogging – are added to

24 An uncommon survival is this former carriage house, reached off Bachelor's Acre but serving a house in the High Street and built in the late nineteenth century.

25 At about the same time as the middle-class houses in Clarence Crescent were being built, slightly less salubrious housing was provided for the artisan classes. This is Albert Street, in Clewer Fields. Such houses have usually been changed far more over the years than the larger ones. The two-storey terraced houses at least have a spacious road between them – now taken over largely by that voracious space-usurper – the motor car.

26 Another lively neo-Gothic front, on 67 Victoria Street, is dated 1888. The door has been altered, but at least an attempt was made to play along with the general characteristics of the over-the-top decoration. This was clearly the show front, with a passageway on the left leading to the yard and workshops behind.

replace decayed wattle and daub panels in old timber-framed buildings. In the Horsehoe Cloister it seems that the builders didn't quite trust the new-fangled technology and adopted a 'bib-and-braces' approach.

It was really in the prosperous later Stuart period that brick began to take a hold in Windsor. The bricks used were invariably a rich red colour, seen, for example on the Guild-hall contrasting admirably with the light-coloured stone dressings. Only much later, from the early nineteenth century onwards, did the much more common yellowy-brown London Stock bricks begin to dominate. For a time, early in the century, there was a fashion to cover brickwork with render, lined to look like finely coursed ashlared stone. This 'stucco' could also be applied directly to timber framing, of course, and, in Windsor as elsewhere, often was.

In much of Windsor's later suburbs, the predominant brick

27 Old Bank House towards the lower end of Thames Street is a dignified late eighteenth-century detached house of seven bays, the middle three projecting slightly and topped by a pediment. In the early nineteenth century it belonged to Richard Ramsbottom, a brewer, and remained in the hands of members of that trade until recently. For many years it was used as offices by Courage.

28 Behind 4 Park Street is this rare example of a surviving backyard complete with outbuildings, once such a common feature of any medieval town. Most of those in Windsor have been swept away and modernized, taking away a little of the town's character in the process.

colour is yellow – or, technically, 'white'. This base colour is usually decorated with bricks of other colours, particularly red bricks used for door and window surrounds. Blues and blacks were also used in moderation to create quite elaborate patterns. In the later nineteenth century, the development of moulded terracotta decoration led to widespread use of this material – particularly on working-class houses.

At the start of Victoria's reign it was said of Windsor that 'considerable improvements have lately been made, among which are the removal of ancient edifices of lath and plaster, and the erection of some handsome ranges of building fronted

30 Fairlight, built in 1885, is one of many large Victorian houses built on Frances Road. Built of brick and detailed in stone, its architectural motifs are mixed and mysterious – but the house certainly has character. Like many such houses, it is simply too big for modern-day families. In this case it has been converted into an hotel; others have been converted into apartments or, a little too often for the social balance of the town, into offices.

with stone.' The use of brick for buildings was particularly admired and 'several in the more modern parts of the town are handsome and well built'. Throughout her reign tastes changed and by the end there was a marked revival in the appreciation of historic buildings, and a far more critical view of their replacements. According to John Murray, writing at the start of this century, the old houses in Windsor had been 'deplorably neglected, and common place buildings had supplanted many old houses in the High Street'. He was more scathing of the then recent developments, claiming that 'few suburbs are less attractive than those which have grown up round this splendid medieval centre'. Those stock-brick terraces that he despised – particularly in Clewer Fields, have gone through years of being looked down upon but now seem to be appreciated far more in an era when too many new buildings have so little character.

31 Uses for some houses have yet to be found and many Victorian buildings in Windsor have been lost – or, like this one of a pair of semis, 33 Osborne Road, are derelict and awaiting an uncertain fate. It would be a shame to see a further erosion of Windsor's nineteenth-century streetscapes – especially as the replacements have almost invariably been exceedingly dull and lifeless.

The early twentieth century brought some fine Edwardian buildings to the town, and in particular to its suburbs, many of which are pompous and overbearing but others definitely have a certain refreshing quality of their own. Many were very large houses indeed, built by very wealthy people – and houses in parts of Windsor are still exceptionally expensive to buy. Since the start of the twentieth century, however, the architecture of Windsor has been little different from that of any other town in the Home Counties. The exception to the rule is the architecture of the Crown Estates; in general, the

32 Park Street, once the main road out of Windsor but blocked in the mid-nineteenth century, is the best Georgian street in the town. All is not quite what it seems though, as some of the buildings are clever reproductions of early twentieth-century date.

housing built for estate workers has been a little more distinctive.

Windsor's planners were at the vanguard of conservation when, between 1959 and 1961, they introduced a face-lift scheme for the High Street – encouraging householders and shop owners to brighten up their facades in an acceptable manner that enhanced the historic character of their buildings. Over the years, too, more and more streets have been stripped of soulless concrete and tarmacadam, and have been resurfaced with cobbles or stone, bringing much needed texture to the streetscape. Presently, and not without some controversy, more of the town centre, including Peascod Street, is being pedestrianized.

Unfortunately, despite these efforts, it has to be said that the second half of the twentieth century has done little to enhance this historic borough. More old buildings – many of which were, admittedly, of only mediocre architectural quality – have been demolished and replaced by new buildings that are even less so. In too many cases, little thought has been given to the

choice of material or the scale of the new build – and the dull, black-brick, monolithic office complex with its steep-sided, duo-pitched, lead-sheeted roof stands cheek-by-jowl with the elegant red-brick Georgian town house. Already these modern materials have become stained and in some cases even covered with lichen. One particularly glaring example of insensitive planning is in the mainly early nineteenth-century development around Holy Trinity Church. One entire quadrant of this area has been completely devastated by the construction of what is now East Berkshire College – a typically uncompromising

34 Always divided up into several shops, with living quarters above, this terrace on St Leonard's Road probably dates back to the turn of the century. The red brick is decorated with terracotta panels, the overall design vaguely reminiscent of the seventeenth century. Several of the original shop-fronts survive more or less intact.

35 Consort House, on Victoria Street, typifies all that was wrong with the architecture of the 1960s and '70s. The bricks are too dark and dull, the concrete completely lifeless; ugly staining has affected both. The design is bland and oppressive, the scale is inhuman, and the ground floor area depressingly dark.

36 Morgan House, not far from Consort House on Madeira Walk, opened in 1991 and shows what can be done with modern buildings. Bright and light, well proportioned, articulated and with interesting details, there is a hint of the commercial work of the innovative late nineteenth-century architect, Richard Norman Shaw. Above all, it fits its place, by the side of the open space of Bachelor's Acre.

'sixties' shoebox' built with no thought for its neighbours. Worse still lies just outside the core of the medieval town.

The grandly named Ward Royal, built in the mid-1960s, comes as a real shock to the system. This huge, low and rational grey concrete complex of flats and ramps and stairways is the sort of thing usually found in some cash-starved inner city borough. It has no organic relationship to the town at all, and no sympathy with the basic human need for individuality and dignity. The pale concrete and brick is already badly marked by wind and weather – and the vandals' spray paint. If ever there was an archetypal architectural carbuncle, this surely has to be it. In mitigation, perhaps Ward Royal should be seen in the context of its period – and after all, it did receive a coveted Civic Trust Award. Fortunately, times, and tastes, change.

Concrete and glass offer tremendous aesthetic possibilities to the modern architect, possibilities undreamed of by their predecessors – but only in a few cases have these been taken advantage of in Windsor. In a backlash against the post-war Modernist movements, the past decade has seen the revival of older styles but – bar a few notable exceptions, mostly done in a rather tacky, cheapskate way – only posterity can safely judge the pseudo-vernacular or the parallel Post-Modernist style.

Despite all this, Windsor still has more than its fair share of historic buildings, even excepting its castle. It is, after all, quite a small town. The castle and the Great Park are more or less sacrosanct and thus free of the threat of changes – bar those enforced by the recent fire. Unfortunately, outside the castle walls the town's planners clearly have to cope with tremendous pressures to redevelop. The close proximity to – and excellent communications with – the capital and Heathrow airport, and the popularity of the town itself, make this inevitable. Fortunately, Windsor's status as a major tourist centre should help to protect at least those well-known buildings and streets in the centre – but there is always the threat of a continual erosion of the relatively unappreciated architectural legacy of the suburbs. One vitally important element in this continuous battle to protect this heritage is public pressure – embodied in this case by the Windsor and Eton Society, founded shortly after the Second World War, uniting the concerns of both towns, and still going strong.

Castle and Defences

The typical Norman castle consisted of a man-made mound, or motte, on top of which was the fighting tower, or keep – the last line of defence. Below the motte was a bailey, an enclosure defended by a ditch and palisade in which all the various lodgings, kitchens and stables could be built. The chalk escarpment chosen by William the Conqueror for the castle at New Windsor was long and narrow, and this allowed a slight change to the typical Norman castle layout. Instead of just one bailey, there were two, and the plan of this first castle is still fossilized in the present arrangement. The Round Tower tops the huge motte, thrown up in between the two baileys. The higher, and more important, of the two baileys is the Upper Ward. The larger but lower bailey is the Lower Ward, but because it was a little more difficult to defend, it was given an extra line of defence and the upper portion became the Middle Ward.

As with most early Norman castles, this first castle was made entirely of timber – with timber-framed buildings and timber defences. The main reasons for this were the need to build swiftly in order to ensure that the castle was ready as soon as possible. Once it could be defended, the more leisurely work of rebuilding it in stone could begin. At Windsor this process took a surprisingly long time, and it was not until almost a century after the Conquest, in the reign of Henry II, that the king could enjoy the, perhaps dubious, delights of a palace built of stone. This was in the Upper Ward, while there were new stone buildings in the Lower Ward for state and

1 The first stone mural towers were designed to help defend the curtain walls, offering flanking fire against anyone trying to scale or undermine them. This particular tower is actually a nineteenth-century copy, on a piece of Wyattville's work near the Round Tower.

ceremonial affairs. The stone itself was a strong chalk, unlike the local softer variety, and came mainly from Totternhoe in Bedfordshire. It probably cost more to transport it the fifty or so miles by wagon than it did to quarry. Local chalk was used in the infilling of the walls and Heath stone, a type of sarsen found lying on or close to the surface in an area about 10 miles or so to the south, was found to be virtually wind- and weather-proof and was used extensively as facing stone.

Towards the end of Henry's reign the first real threat to the crown came not from his subjects but from within his own royal house – intrigues stirred up by his own sons, Richard and John. As a result, a programme of replacing the timber defences around Windsor Castle began, beginning with the

1 The first Norman castle was centred on a huge man-made mound, or motte, between the two wards, topped by a timber keep or fighting tower. This was replaced by a stone-shell keep – the Round Tower – by Henry II in the twelfth century. Its present distinctive appearance is the result of Wyattville's remodelling in 1831 when it was raised over 30 ft higher, and refaced and battlemented.

Upper Ward and the tower on the motte. The new Round Tower that replaced the original fighting tower on the motte was a type of structure called a shell keep. Essentially it consisted of a circular stone wall and buildings were built inside it against the wall. Much of this work still remains, though the external appearance of the tower is only one hundred and fifty or so years old. The defensive walls were given projecting square towers – mural towers – typical of the twelfth century. Again, much of this work survives, particularly in the outer walls of the Upper Ward.

The work continued into the Middle Ward and along the sides of the Lower Ward, but the rest of the defences were still only made of timber when the two ungrateful sons of the late King Henry began quarrelling among themselves after his death. The first siege of the castle in 1194 ended when they temporarily patched up their differences.

In 1216 the stone defences were still unfinished when there was a much longer siege – the second and the last. John, by now king, had broken the agreements with the barons enshrined in Magna Carta and the barons, not surprisingly, rebelled. John's forces inside Windsor, under the command of Engelard de Cigogne, were besieged by an army led by the Count de Nevers. For three months the defenders held out until the seige was lifted. The attackers had found out that whilst they were held up at Windsor, John's forces were devastating their unprotected estates elsewhere in the country.

The stone walls around the Lower Ward were completed in the reign of Henry III, when the advantages of the round, rather than square, mural tower had been realized – hence the shape of the much rebuilt Clewer, Garter's and Salisbury Towers on the western section of the curtain wall. The Clewer Tower still has its dingy, depressing dungeon. Henry made the castle one of his main residences and set about radically rebuilding the accommodation within the walls during the 1240s. As well as building new royal lodgings in the Lower Ward, he also built a new chapel and a cloister near to them, fragments of which still remain within later buildings.

A century later, most of Henry's domestic buildings – in their day no doubt some of the finest in the kingdom – were swept away by his great grandson, Edward III. Edward's main

interests in life were war and pageantry, and he pursued both with considerable vigour. He dragged England into the quite pointless Hundred Years War with France and, although not a particularly brilliant tactician himself, he was fortunate to have serving him men who were. Great victories at Sluys (1340), Crecy (1346) and Poitiers (1356) brought him glory, and the country to the brink of starvation. In 1348, following a series of huge tournaments, he founded the famous Order of the Garter at Windsor, and a new College of Canons to care for the souls of these military knights.

Edward was, according to one source, 'besy and corious in bildyng' and, after a two-year delay caused by the outbreak of the Black Death, his chivalric ideals began to be enshrined in stone. Many kinds of stone, in fact, brought to Windsor mainly from Taynton in Oxfordshire and Reigate in Surrey, but also

1 The classic, tourist, picture-postcard view of Windsor Castle, looking up the grand approach drive with one of the splendid horse-drawn carriages available for hire. The principal feature in the view is Henry VIII's Great Gatehouse, finished in 1516 by the mason, Henry Smyth.

from as far afield as Somerset, Lincolnshire and even Yorkshire.
Other building materials included hundreds of oak trees, huge
amounts of lead and even some sea coal shipped from County
Durham to fire the furnaces of the blacksmiths. The king
empowered his officials to obtain any materials they thought fit,
and the transport to carry it. He also sent officials out into the
country to attract, persuade or force the best craftsmen of the day
to come to Windsor. Sometimes, their masters had to be
threatened if they tried to stop them going. At one time there
were some two hundred and sixty masons at work in the castle,
paid the then handsome sum of 6*d* per day, as well as carpenters,
glaziers, plasterers, sawyers, lime-burners and a host of general
labourers. It was said at the time that no one else could then build
anything remotely ambitious elsewhere in the country, because
all the skilled men were working in the castle. The master mason
in charge of the work was initially John de Sponlee, who was
replaced in 1361 by William Wynford – one of the most famous
of his day. William Herland was in charge of the carpentry.

The old Chapel of St Edward in the Lower Ward was
refurbished and reroofed to become the chapel of the new
order, rededicated to Our Lady, St Edward and St George, and
new cloisters were built to its north to house the college. The
inside of the Round Tower on the motte was completely
rebuilt, the present King John's Tower was added and, to cater
for all the additional people either living in or visiting the
castle, new lodgings were built against the inside of the south
and east walls of the Upper Ward. The centre-piece of the new
building in the Upper Ward was the great St George's Hall,
built in line with an existing private chapel to house the great
feasting occasions in which Edward delighted.

King Edward died in 1377 and work on the castle virtually
stopped. Windsor was still a royal palace, though, and
Geoffrey Chaucer, the great medieval poet, knew it well. A
civil servant, to all intents and purposes, he was commissioned
in 1390 to take care of the repairs that were already needed to
the Chapel of St George. It is quite possible that he was
thinking of Windsor when, in the 'Knight's Tale', he writes of
a 'paleys ful of pepul up and doun' that had a 'grete tour'. The
civil unrest at the end of the century and the renewal of
hostilities with France meant little more work was done on the

1 A detail of the twelfth-
century masonry close
by the so-called 'Norman
Gate' reveals the use of
galletting – pieces of flint
embedded into the
mortar fixing of the
stone blocks while it was
still wet. In this case, this
was almost certainly just
for ornament rather than
for straightening the
coursing or for added
strength.

1 General improvements in military defences led to the development of rounded towers, better able to resist undermining by attackers. The masonry defences facing Thames Street were built by Henry III. On the right is the Garter Tower, and to the left, the Clewer Tower, given its present almost French appearance by Salvin in the 1860s. Within it is a dingy, vaulted dungeon, occasionally open to the public.

castle and it began to decay again. By 1457 it was reported that many roofs were leaking so badly that parts of the castle 'be fallen in grete and ruynouse decay'.

Two years before, the first real event in what became known as the Wars of the Roses took place. In 1471 the Yorkist King Edward IV overthrew the Lancastrian King Henry VI for the second time and within a few years felt sufficiently confident to start a new phase of building at Windsor. This mainly consisted of building the new and magnificent St George's Chapel immediately to the west of the old, and the new Horsehoe Cloister nearby to rehouse the canons.

Although the infamous Richard III was a patron of the arts, he reigned only a short time before being defeated at Bosworth

1 Just inside Henry VIII's Great Gatehouse are the rebuilt lodgings of the Poor Knights; these were paid for out of the king's will and built mainly of material salvaged from one of the many religious houses that he plundered – in this case, Reading Abbey, just up river. To the left is the Mary Tudor Tower, home of the governor of the Military Knights. This part of the castle was heavily restored by Edward Blore in the mid-nineteenth century.

by the first of the Tudor monarchs, Henry VII. Henry mainly concentrated on finishing the work in progress, though he did extend the royal apartments in the Upper Ward westwards to the Inner Gate – now known, oddly and inaccurately, as the Norman Gate. It was his son, the much-married Henry VIII, who made the next major contribution to Windsor. Soon after he came to the throne he ordered the Great Gatehouse – until recently the public entrance – to be built. It took the mason Henry Smyth six years, and was completed by 1516. The gatehouse was designed more for show than defence, with exaggerated machicolations over a gateway flanked by proud half-octagonal towers. Its crisp appearance today is a result of a nineteenth-century refacing.

In his will, Henry also gave money to rehouse thirteen of the Poor Knights attached to the College of St George and their new lodgings were built close to the Great Gateway in the 1550s. Appropriately enough, much of the masonry used was

1 Apart from a handful of rooms inside the state apartments of the Upper Ward, there is little obvious survival of the radical remodelling of the castle carried out by Hugh May for Charles II. The Henry III Tower retains the odd windows May devised in the 1670s – a cross between the medieval originals and the neoclassical. All the others in the castle were removed by Wyatt or Wyattville when the taste for a purer Gothic style reasserted itself.

plundered from the ruins of Reading Abbey – one of the many religious houses that fell victim to Henry's dissolution of the monasteries. Despite this work, the castle was yet again in poor condition and the Marquess of Windsor wrote in 1559 that 'reparacions must needes be doon at Windsoure . . . before the queenes majestie come there'. Elizabeth I added a new gallery but little else, apart from general maintenance and some internal redecoration, took place at Windsor for over a century. In the Civil War the castle was used as a military base for the Parliament and as a prison for Royalist troops. The most famous prisoner of all was King Charles himself, brought to the castle just before Christmas 1648. After his execution in the new year, his body was brought back to Windsor and carried through the Lower Ward in a snowfall to be buried, in silence, in St George's Chapel.

The temporarily redundant palace was described a few years later by John Evelyn as 'large in circumfrence, but the roomes Melancholy & of antient Magnificence' and all in all the castle was 'exceedingly ragged and ruinous'. It was, in fact, on the verge of falling down by the time Charles II returned to reclaim his throne in 1660. The exiled king had seen the magnificent palaces of France and particularly admired the one recently built at Versailles by Louis Le Vau for Louis XIV. Back in England, he set about trying to emulate his French cousin.

In 1674 Hugh May, appointed comptroller of the king's works the year before, began a ten-year-long transformation of the crumbling castle. The ramshackle medieval buildings along the north side of the Upper Ward were either knocked down or radically rebuilt, and a new structure – the Star Building – added, fronting a widened terrace. Round-headed Italianate windows, mostly in Portland stone, replaced the pointed Gothic ones in other parts of the castle and the internal arrangements were radically altered. Indeed, it was inside that the real splendour of the new work shone. The celebrated Venetian artist, Antonio Verrio, painted many of the ceilings, whilst the Englishman, Grinling Gibbons, carved exquisite panels. The work cost over £130,000 – a staggering amount for the time. Most of this was to be swept away in the nineteenth century, but three rooms retain much of their late seventeenth-century appearance – the Queen's Presence Chamber, the Queen's Audience Chamber and the King's Dining Room. It has to be said that the full-blown Baroque style so admired by Charles after his stay in France has always been a little too rich for the English architectural palate – and these rooms are reminders of this. Nevertheless, the quality of the surviving craftsmanship has to be admired.

For virtually all of the eighteenth century, the castle was merely maintained. The first two Hanoverian kings appear to have had little love for the place and it was only at the end of

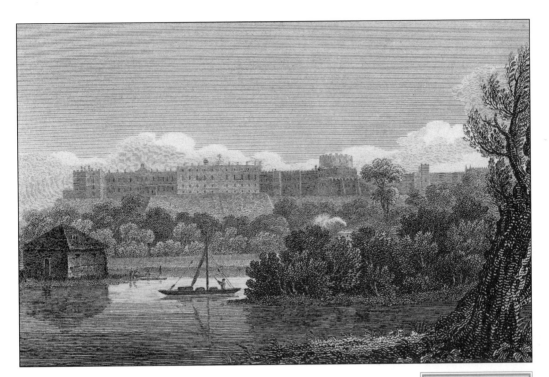

his long reign that George III began to take an interest. Such was the condition of the castle itself, the king and his family had to stay in a house just outside the walls. Gradually the buildings were made habitable – and from 1800 onwards the fashionable architect, James Wyatt, set about rebuilding the castle in the Gothic style. All this was totally eclipsed in the short reign of the extravagant George IV.

That king, who gave us the renowned Brighton Pavilion, had always been keen on the romance of Windsor and wanted the by now varied collection of buildings to evoke once again the medieval splendour of the place. In 1824 a competition to find the right man to do this was won by Jeffry Wyatt, James Wyatt's nephew. In August, the king laid the foundation stone of the new work and sanctioned Wyatt to change his name to Wyattville. In the next few years the original estimate of £150,000 rose to around £1,000,000 as the castle assumed its present shape. Medieval walls were refaced and towers restored; windows and doorways all became Gothic; and the buildings in the Upper Ward were radically altered inside and out. The domestic quarters of the royal family were moved from the north side of the ward to the south and east sides, the north side being remodelled into the state apartments, centred on a completely rebuilt St George's Hall. May's work and Verrio's decoration were largely swept aside and the whole thing was redone in the late Gothic style. The length of the hall was increased by incorporating the older private chapel next to it.

By the end of 1828 the first phase of the remodelling was finished. In December the king was able to move in to the new palatial royal lodgings around the sides of the Upper Ward – and Wyattville was knighted by his delighted client. The architect's master stroke came in the second phase of work. In 1831, the Great, or Round, Tower on top of the motte was completely recased and raised 30 ft or so. This gave the castle a dominant focal point that tied all its other remodelled and refaced elements together in what is, from a distance, a Romantic masterpiece. Closer up, it has to be said, the finish leaves quite a bit to be desired. The detailing of the new work is rather mechanical, everything a little too crisp, and the unnatural black mortar is distinctly off-putting and quite unattractive. Nevertheless, Windsor Castle had achieved the form that has since graced many a calendar, biscuit-tin lid and postcard – and George IV and Wyattville had achieved their goal. Later changes have been comparatively minimal, mainly associated with restoration.

At present a major programme of work is once again under way – but this is not the result of royal whim or essential repair. On 20 November 1992 fire roared through much of the Upper Ward, badly damaging the buildings between the Grand Reception Room and the Chester Tower. Among the other rooms affected were Wyattville's St George's Hall, the Crimson and Green Drawing Rooms, the private chapel, and the Brunswick and Prince of Wales Towers. Most of the decorative schemes destroyed were Wyattville's, but the earlier Hugh May and medieval fabric still surviving behind the later gilt and plaster were also badly affected. Almost immediately work began on shoring the fabric, clearing the debris in a delicate

archaeological operation, and planning its reconstruction. Hopes were raised that the restored portions would contribute a little of the late twentieth-century style to the castle, but a more conservative approach has been adopted. The huge cost of the repairs has also led directly to the imposition of admission charges to the grounds for the first time and, indirectly, to the queen opening up Buckingham Palace to the public to raise more funds. By the end of 1993 the new steel roof trusses over the hall were in place and work is proceeding apace.

Windsor Castle, despite its homogeneous appearance, has elements dating from the eleventh to the late twentieth centuries, and it is both one of the oldest continuously inhabited royal palaces in the world, and the largest and most influential example of nineteenth-century Romantic architectural taste.

1 The Upper Ward is, superficially, all early nineteenth-century work – but encases much older masonry. On the left, in front of Wyattville's huge *porte-cochère*, is part of the late fifteenth-century work of Edward IV, refaced by James Wyatt. On the same side beyond the *porte-cochère* is the fire-ravaged St George's Hall, now being repaired. The other two sides of the courtyard are entirely by Wyattville, who added new walls parallel to the existing medieval ones to allow room for a grand corridor all around this part of the ward.

37 The inside of St John's is completely different from that of St George's Chapel. While it may lack medieval grandeur and opulence of decoration, it has its own individual charm – a certain delicacy of design and a deftness of architectural touch. The slender piers supporting the galleries, and the roof trusses echoing the later Middle Ages, are all of iron.

Churches

The most magnificent specimen of ecclesiastic architecture in Windsor, and, indeed, one that can claim to be one of the best in Britain, is, technically, only a chapel. When Edward III founded his Order of the Garter in 1348 he restored the mid-thirteenth-century chapel built by Henry III in the Lower Ward. This became the order's chapel and was rededicated to Our Lady, St Edward and St George – though usually known simply as St George's. There was also a chapter house nearby for the order, built by 1352; remains of its ground floor were later incorporated into the deanery, probably rebuilt when Dean Wren, the father of Sir Christopher, was the incumbent.

Connected with the religious buildings, and tucked away behind the present chapel, are two small cloisters. The Dean's Cloisters were originally added by Henry III in the 1240s. The south walk wall, the door to the chapel and a fine but fading wall-painting – possibly of Edward the Confessor – survive from that period. It was subsequently rebuilt by Edward III in an equally grand manner. Edward also built the Canons' Cloister, originally with timber-framed lodgings for the canons and vicars surrounding it. As their numbers fell the buildings changed and the individual houses grew larger.

In the aftermath of the Wars of the Roses, the victorious Yorkist king, Edward IV, decided to build a new, and much grander, chapel. Across the Thames his Lancastrian predecessor, Henry VI, had begun the chapel of his college at Eton in 1448. This, even now, towers over the flat river meadows despite the tree-growth and the discordant clutter of the twentieth century. The view from the castle's North Terrace gives some impression of how it must have appeared to Edward IV – the crisp new building must have put the small chapel within the castle to shame.

In 1477 Edward allowed the old great hall and vicars' lodgings in the Lower Ward to be swept away, and work started on the new St George's. The architect, or master mason, was Henry Janyns, who had worked at Eton. When Edward died, in 1483, the great choir was finished, covered by a temporary wooden roof, but the transepts were only half-built and the nave scarcely started. After the infamous Richard III was overthrown by Henry VII in 1485 work on the chapel stopped. It was restarted in the early 1490s but carried on quite lethargically; the final section of vaulting was not finished until 1528. Several changes were made to the design in the process – the attached chapels were raised higher, the planned crossing tower abandoned and, most significantly, the nave was lengthened by a bay, and a magnificent new west end and window added. In charge of much of this later work, including most of the vaulting,

38 Close up the grandeur of St George's and the degree of decoration becomes even more impressive – heraldry and humour frozen in stone. The necessary patching and repairs of recent restorations also become evident, but will weather down in time. The fine King's Beasts only date from the 1920s – but reflect medieval ancestors taken down by Wren in the seventeenth century.

38 The magnificent interior of the choir of St George's, seen in a Victorian drawing. The flat vaulting that fascinated Celia Fiennes three hundred years ago is still an engineering miracle – a supreme example of the confidence of the medieval mason. Above the canopied choir stalls, carved between 1477 and 1485, are each knight's 'achievements' – his sword, helm, banner and crest.

38 St George's Chapel in the Lower Ward of the castle is one of the finest specimens of Perpendicular Gothic in the world. Begun in 1477 this chapel – and it is only a chapel – was not finished until 1528. Whether by accident or design it managed to combine medieval grandeur and display with the symmetry and proportion of the Renaissance. Cherished and restored as it is, and needing constant maintenance, it is nevertheless a shame to see such an insensitively sited bookshop – surely it could be put somewhere else?

39 The deanery, built close to the east end of the first St George's Chapel, was remodelled when Sir Christopher Wren's father was dean. The range to the left contains substantial remains of the Order of the Garter's Chapter House, built around 1350.

38 Rebuilt and remodelled for a succession of would-be occupiers, the Lady chapel still contains elements of the first St George's Chapel built in the mid-thirteenth century and remodelled when the Order of the Garter was founded in 1348. Most of the chapel was rebuilt from 1494 but remained virtually unused for centuries. In the 1860s it was chosen as Prince Albert's memorial chapel and radically redecorated inside. The fact that this work was confined to the interior is fortunate – the decor is somewhat overpoweringly sumptuous.

was William Vertue, perhaps the finest mason of his day. The money for it came not from Henry, but from a bequest by one of his closest friends, Sir Reginald Bray, who died in 1503.

The overall result is one of the most splendid examples of that peculiarly English version of Gothic architecture – the Perpendicular. In fact, St George's is the last great example of the style, and certain elements of the design anticipate Tudor forms and the influence of the Renaissance. It has, for example, a remarkably symmetrical southern 'show' front for a medieval church, with the apsidal end of the south transept

40 Clewer church, St Andrew's, still manages to appear a typical village church, surrounded by its graveyard, despite the close proximity of the relief road and suburban semis. There was a church here long before the castle was begun, though the oldest part of the present building was probably started at the same time. This view is from the north.

forming a centre-piece matched by the chapels at either end. Inside, the dominant feature is the flattish 'four-centred' arch favoured by the Tudors, and there is also a feeling of width as well as height – helped by the fact that the choir is as wide as the nave. Light floods through the huge windows and the whole interior is a riot of baronial colour and magnificence – and the almost flat vaulting a quite astonishing piece of medieval engineering. Nearly two hundred years after it was built Celia Fiennes was quite fascinated by it, writing that 'the rooff . . . is very curious carv'd stone and soe thinn to the leads one might grasp it between thumb and finger – and yet so well fixt. as to be very strong'.

The chapel has, inevitably, needed to be repaired over the years. Commonwealth troops desecrated the interior and plundered its riches in the Civil War. In the early 1680s Christopher Wren, whose father was the Dean of Windsor, inspected the fabric and found it to be in urgent need of

40 In the late 1850s St Andrew's Church was restored by Henry Woodyer, who also added this splendidly eccentric lych-gate – built in flint with brick and stone decoration. The timber forest supporting the open part of the roof is unique – and perhaps not surprisingly so!

remedial work. He carried out repairs to the roof and also found that the famous King's Beasts on top of the buttresses were dangerous and so had them removed. A century later Henry Emlyn restored the chapel for George III, who spent £20,000 on the work. Emlyn, a carpenter by trade, added new pews and stalls that blend superbly with the old – though the original east window was removed and replaced with a rather garish painted one, designed by Benjamin West. The magnificent west window – one of the largest of its kind in the world – almost suffered the same fate but survived and was restored in 1842 by Thomas Willement. In the 1860s Sir George Gilbert Scott restored parts of the chancel, reconstructed the east window in its medieval form and added the grand ceremonial flight of steps at the west end. Later, throughout most of the 1880s, John Pearson added new buttresses and embattled parapets.

Unfortunately, the chapel needed yet more work. In 1918 Sir

Harold Brakspear reported that the eighteenth-century repairs had simply not attacked the real problems. As *The Times* put it a few years later, the Georgian builders had 'applied tenpennyworth of plaster and pretence instead of pounds' worth of stone and common sense and trusted to luck and posterity to make good King Henry VII's shortcomings and its own parsimonious procrastinations'.

Another major restoration began under Brakspear's supervision in 1920, during which the roof and vaults of the choir and nave were repaired and seventy-six copies of the the original King's Beasts, carved by Joseph Armytage, were put

37 A detail of one of the Gothick doorways of St John's Church.

41 Holy Trinity Church opened in 1844 and was partly built to be the town's garrison church. Built of brick, to the designs of Edward Blore, it is a fairly plain but spiky neo-Gothic pile. Later additions to it have not been very sympathetic to the overall design, but the church sits well at the end of each of the roads leading up to it.

back in place. During this work, the chapel's inadequate foundations, which had caused problems for over four hundred years, were finally dealt with. Buttresses were added to the north and south transepts, blending in splendidly with the medieval work, and existing buttresses were repaired or practically replaced. The chancel was reopened in 1927 and work then moved to the nave. The official reopening of the chapel took place in November 1930, in the presence of George V. The whole job cost about £175,000 – money raised by the Crown, the Knights of the Garter, and private donations. Apart from the treasures associated with the Order of the Garter – the banners, shields and the garter stall plates – the chapel boasts a magnificent set of carved stalls as well as the second largest number of carved misericords in England; ninety-six examples of medieval life in miniature. The

misericord is a small, tilt-up seat which, even in the 'up' position, has a carved rest just at the right height to allow its occupant to rest his bottom on it when supposedly standing during the often interminable services of the medieval church. The three tiers of stalls and the misericords were probably made in London between 1477 and 1483 under the supervision of the master carver, William Berkeley. The replacements and additions of Emlyn in the late eighteenth century are so good that they would be difficult to spot without a guidebook.

Henry VII took an interest in the unfinished St George's Chapel because he had decided to be buried at Windsor. The old and now redundant chapel next to it was chosen as the site for a new Lady chapel that would house his mortal remains. Most of the masonry was pulled down, leaving only the Galilee chapel, with its three original doorways, and parts of the north wall. On the outside, this faces the rebuilt cloisters and still has its original

43 In 1853 Henry Woodyer began work on the House of Mercy in Hatch Lane, Clewer – an exceedingly dull, brick, Gothic pile that simply grew and grew. This rare piece of decorative extravagance is over the main entrance of what is now the Convent of St John the Baptist.

43 More than twenty years after he started the House of Mercy, Woodyer added this long range in 1874. The good work that the charity did is not reflected in its forbidding architecture. The portion to the right was added as recently as the 1920s.

Purbeck marble columns attached to it. The new Lady chapel was of the same dimensions as the old and was started in 1494, though not finished at Henry's death in 1509. The canons of Windsor managed to finish the chapel by 1514. One of their number was Thomas Wolsey, who, as Cardinal Wolsey, was given the chapel and planned to be buried there. However Wolsey fell from grace after arguing with Henry VIII. The king also decided to be buried in the chapel and, likewise, was destined not to be – he was buried in the new St George's instead.

The old chapel, known for years as Wolsey's Tomb House, thus remained without any real purpose and gradually decayed. James II is said to have converted it into a Roman Catholic chapel in the late 1680s – to the anger of the locals – but it was then abandoned again for over a century. George III ordered a royal crypt to be built beneath it in 1804, which was used but the chapel above remained neglected until the 1860s. Then it was radically redecorated in a rather alarming manner out of keeping with all the other Gothic work in the castle walls by the Baron de Trinqueti – having been chosen as a memorial chapel to Prince Albert by his grief-stricken widow.

For an ancient town that has played such a prominent role in the affairs of the nation, Windsor has a remarkable paucity of old churches outside the castle walls. Indeed, only one church is more than two centuries old – aptly enough the church of Clewer, the parish out of which New Windsor was carved shortly after the Conquest. Despite being swamped by the rapid expansion of Windsor in the late nineteenth century, the church and churchyard still give the impression of being at the centre of a quiet English village. The present church of St Andrew's was built at about the same time as work started on the new castle nearby. Built mainly of flint, it retains some typical round-arched Norman windows and its original chancel arch, but was altered around about 1400 when the clerestorey was added. At the west end is a low tower topped by a broach spire.

In 1858 the church was restored by Henry Woodyer, a friend of William Butterfield, but with little of that radical Gothic revivalist's flair. His work on the church itself was relatively restrained, concentrating on the rebuilding of the north arcade and on repairing the exterior. The architect then let himself go completely the lodge and lych-gate to the churchyard. This

little composition is quite remarkable, not to say eccentric – particularly with regard to the roof over the gateway itself supported on a bizarre array of braced timbers. The lodge now houses a small local history museum.

The official parish church of Windsor lies on the High Street, not far from the castle, and the first church, dedicated to St John the Baptist, was in existence by the early twelfth century. By the early nineteenth century the old medieval building was described as 'a spacious, ancient but ill-built fabric'. Repairs did little to improve matters, so the decision was made to demolish and build anew – at an estimated cost of around £9,000. The architect chosen for the task was Charles Hollis, with Jeffry Wyattville acting as an advisor. Work started in 1820, and by the time it was finished two years later, the cost had soared to £14,040 17*s* 3*d*.

The design was an embattled variation of Regency Gothic –

a style neoclassical in everything except its debased copies of details derived from many different medieval (and, in this case, Tudor) periods. The crisp, light-coloured ashlar suits it well. Inside, it is light and airy, with a gallery round three sides of the nave supported by thin cast-iron columns. The traceried roof trusses are also of iron, then a fairly novel material in church building. Shortly after it was built it was described as 'a handsome structure in the later style of English architecture'. Slightly later, when the more serious Gothic Revival was at its height, this much more cheerful church was described as 'a spacious building, of poor modern design'.

The chancel was rebuilt between 1869 and 1873 by Samuel Sanders Teulon, in that typical mid-Victorian Gothic way. The result is ponderous and predictable and unbalances the original design. The surprisingly delicate, carved chancel

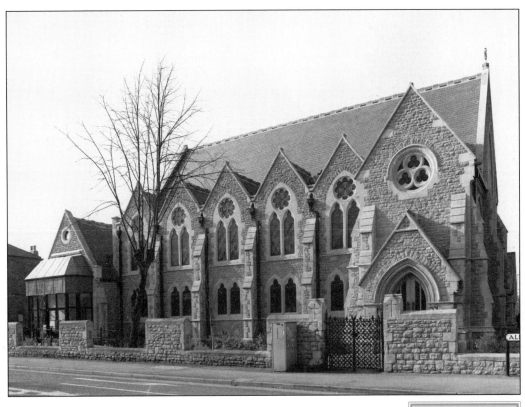

46 Only a short distance along Alma Road from the new Roman Catholic church is this Methodist chapel probably built at around the same time. Without the signs, it would be difficult to distinguish between the building belonging to the Church of Rome and the followers of John Wesley's radical Non-conformism.

screen was added in 1898 by Sir Arthur Blomfield to commemorate Queen Victoria's sixtieth jubilee of the previous year. The main treasure within the church is the railings to the small south chapel off the chancel, carved by Grinling Gibbons in about 1682 and originally in the private chapel in the castle. In the early 1990s the church is again being repaired.

The centre-piece of the new middle-class development being developed by James Bedborough to the south-west of the old town was a new church. Holy Trinity, opened in 1844, was built partly because of pressure from Prince Albert. The architect was Edward Blore, who had been an architectural advisor to William IV and who finished the remodelling of Buckingham Palace in the late 1830s on the Prince Consort's instructions. Set in its own square, the brick church confidently ends each of the planned straight avenues leading towards it. From these viewpoints, it looks considerably better than it does

47 For Henry Woodyer, St Stephen's Church on Vansittart Road is a fairly conventional neo-Gothic edifice with few architectural oddities. Begun in 1870 and partly opened in 1871, it was finished in 1874. It had started as a chapel-of-ease in what was then the slum district of Clewer Fields – but quickly became the centre of a new parish.

on closer inspection. The interior, though, is spacious and galleried. Holy Trinity served an affluent area to which many officers and others associated with the castle were moving; it was also the garrison church.

Later on the Revd Ellison, vicar of Windsor when the chancel was added to St John's, was aware of the lack of free pew space available for the less well-off inhabitants of the rapidly growing town. He began a fund, to which Queen Victoria donated £300, to finance a new church, All Saints, in Frances Road. The queen's favourite daughter, Victoria the Princess Royal, had become Crown princess of Prussia in 1858 and in 1863 laid the foundation stone of the new church while visiting home. It was one of Arthur (later Sir Arthur) Blomfield's earlier churches. Tall and roomy, this high Victorian Gothic pile is of red brick with bold bands of blue on

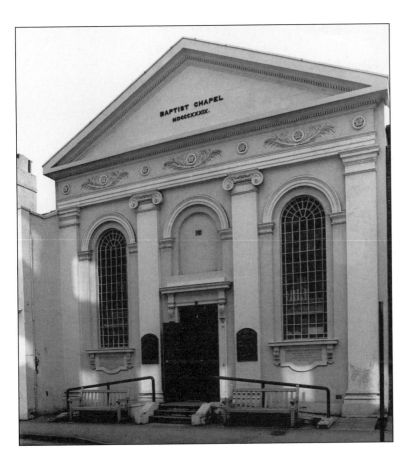

48 The Baptist Chapel on Victoria Street is a more typical Nonconformist design – neoclassical rather than neo-Gothic. Its stuccoed facade is dated 1839 and the details are typically debased – a mixture of Greek Ionic pilasters and Roman Doric – all with a touch of the Italianate. Overall it is pleasant, well-cared for and serves its original purpose.

the outside, and more colourful polychrome brick within. Apart from this decoration it is really quite a plain church, its main ornamental feature being the large, plate-traceried round window at the west end, and a spirelet-topped belfry rising from the east end of the nave. Incidentally, Thomas Hardy, the great poet and novelist, is said to have had a hand in the design of this church as he was working for Butterfield at the time.

Two churches in the Clewer area owe their existence to Mariquita Tennant, the widow of a clergyman. She had sheltered 'fallen women' in her house, The Limes, in Clewer village but was forced to give up because of ill health in 1851. Her work was carried on by Harriet Monsell and a new House of Mercy was founded in Hatch Lane, later becoming the Anglican Convent of St John the Baptist. Henry Woodyer offered his services for nothing and designed the first quadrangle of rather boring Gothic buildings in 1853. The complex has been added to over the years, the last major alterations having taken place in the 1920s. Woodyer's small original chapel was superseded in 1881 by a new one designed, again, by him. In complete contrast to the rest of the convent this new brick church, with its apsed chancel and tall, traceried, gable-topped windows, was a much bolder and more powerful affair that is much more pleasing to the eye.

The convent began to widen their scope of good works by catering to the poor and the needy – of which Victorian Windsor had many – and in the late 1860s opened a new mission in the slum area of Clewer Fields. Woodyer designed another new church, on Vansittart Road, begun in 1870 and opened for worship on 25 July the following year. It was not completed, however, until the end of 1874 – by which time it was the church of a newly created parish. Large and plain, St Stephen's is built of London Stock brick and, it has to be said, borders on the utilitarian and is no architectural masterpiece.

The Roman Catholic community had a chapel of sorts in Hermitage Lane from 1826, when they were still subject to a degree of discrimination and abuse. Changes in the law allowed them the freedom to be more open about their faith and in October 1868 a much larger church opened on Alma Road, dedicated to St Edward the Confessor. The work of a little-known church architect, Charles Alban Buckler, this Gothic Revival church built of rough ragstone cost in the region of £4,000. It has no tower, but a tall clerestorey, and is actually quite striking.

In a rare contrast to the various shades of Gothic elsewhere, the Baptist Chapel in Victoria Street is a refreshing example of the neoclassical. The facade of this 1839 building is dominated by the Ionic pilasters of its attached portico, and it is good to see how the chapel is still catering for the needs of its congregation at the end of the twentieth century – even to the extent of adding ramps for the elderly or disabled that actually fit in quite well with the symmetry of the design. An arguably finer neoclassical chapel, designed by Jesse Hollis in William Street for the Congregational Church in 1832, was sadly demolished in 1979. By that time it had become the United Reformed Church, and the congregation now use premises within the new development on the site.

Public Buildings

Windsor has few public buildings of great antiquity, largely because the town was, until the middle of the last century, quite small and insignificant. As a borough with a market it did need its market house, situated in the High Street. Towards the end of the seventeenth century, at a time of prosperity, the existing market house, built in 1596, was considered to be in need of replacement. Sir Thomas Fitch, a prominent London builder, designed a new building, the Guild-hall, to replace it, and work started under the direction of John Clarke in September 1687. Fitch died soon afterwards and Sir Christopher Wren, by then one of the most celebrated architects in the kingdom, was called in to finish it off.

The building opened in 1689 and cost £2,000. In its layout it continued the traditions of such buildings since the medieval period, with a covered area for the market stalls beneath the meeting rooms on the first floor. Fortunately, unlike so many others, it has the open ground floor as designed, with no insensitive infilling. The design is assuredly classical, with fine use of rich red brick decorated with stone. Tradition has it that when Wren had finished, the good councillors of Windsor were concerned about the wide span of the beams and insisted that he put in additional columns. Wren, confident in its construction, compromised by adding columns that were just a couple of inches too short and the councillors never noticed. Quite how they could fail to notice is another question – but

the columns are, undoubtedly, too short and serve no structural purpose whatsoever.

The statue of Queen Anne in a niche on the west side was added by the townspeople in 1707, although this amiable but none too bright and somewhat gouty monarch was rather more rotund than her effigy would suggest. The statue of her husband, Prince George of Denmark, was added at the opposite end of the building in 1713, at the expense of Wren's son, another Christopher, who was MP for the borough. In June 1829 the foundation stone of a two-bay extension to the Guild-hall was laid, which provided a mayor's parlour and committee room; alterations were also made to the first floor of the original portion.

The oldest surviving purpose-built school buildings in the town were built at what was then the corner of St John's churchyard on Church Lane. The Free School was founded in 1705 to provide education for children – thirty-six boys and

9 Windsor's pleasant late-seventeenth-century town hall was designed by Sir Thomas Fitch but finished, after his death, by Sir Christopher Wren in 1689 – the year after the accession of William and Mary. The inner two rows of columns are superfluous to the design and do not even touch the beams they are meant to be supporting. Folklore has it that they were put in by Wren as a little joke at the expense of the councillors who doubted the solidity of the original design.

49 Almost tucked away out of site on the edge of central Windsor is a fine early eighteenth-century former school, now used as a masonic hall. The architect is unknown, but there is a hint of Wren's influence in its subdued baroque. The Free School was founded in 1705 but this building opened in 1726, remaining a school until 1862.

50 George Edmund Street designed the new Royal Free School and teacher's houses, and they opened in 1862. The brick Gothic must have been quite intimidating to its young students – though it was a style used almost universally during the Victorian period. The school buildings, off Bachelor's Acre, have been disused for some time and are about to be converted into apartments.

thirty-six girls – of the deserving poor of the borough; Queen Anne provided a £50 annual bounty. The new buildings did not open until 1726, and the added impetus was largely the result of a bequest two years earlier in the will of Theodore Randue. The school was designed in bold brick baroque, a style already going out of fashion at the time but a suitable epitaph to the Stuart age. It remained in these undoubtedly handsome quarters until the start of 1862, when it amalgamated with the National School to form the new Royal Free School in new premises on Bachelors Acre. The old buildings were sold and became a masonic hall.

The National School had been founded partly through the efforts of Edward Hawke Locker, a benefactor of the town's poor in the early nineteenth century. The new buildings of the Royal Free School were designed by one of the best architects of the Victorian period, George Edmund Street – who went on to design, among other buildings, the Law Courts in London.

53 In the then poverty-stricken area of Clewer Fields, the efforts of the Clewer Convent led to the building of a church, St Stephen's, and then a school next to it – on Arthur Road. The main school buildings are dated 1876 – and Henry Woodyer was probably the architect involved. The buildings may look rather tatty now, but at the time must have really improved the quality of life in the area.

Street was a keen advocate of the Gothic Revival, and not just for churches, so it had to be the Gothic style for the new school and the teachers' houses. Surprisingly, the material used is brick – Street generally seems to have preferred stone but perhaps that was considered too expensive for such an establishment. The school itself moved out many years ago, and the buildings are disused and in danger of becoming derelict. At the time of writing there are plans to convert the buildings into apartments and, if successful, these will help ensure the survival of a remarkably intact group of attractive Victorian buildings off the otherwise rather bleak Bachelors Acre – the Royal Free School, the former Windsor Almshouses, and Chariott's Charity.

Most of the other Victorian schools, generally associated with churches, were almost invariably also built in the neo-Gothic style – with varied degrees of success. In complete contrast, the

earlier St George's School, at the base of the hill off Datchett Road, is neoclassical. The school was founded by a Mr Travers and was built in 1803. The broad eleven-bay two-storey centre has a fine Doric loggia and pediment and is flanked by three-bay wings.

Windsor had a 'pesthouse' on Sheet Street in the early seventeenth century but in the nineteenth century the sick poor were still badly catered for. This was partly relieved by the Windsor Royal Infirmary in Victoria Street, supported by, among many others, Queen Victoria herself. This was replaced in 1909 by the King Edward VII Memorial Hospital, built slightly away from the town centre in St Leonard's Road and, appropriately enough, possibly near to the site of a medieval leper hospital. The original part of the new hospital was designed by A.W. West. Though stucccoed, it is of a vaguely Queen Anne Revival style, comprising two storeys with attics in the tiled mansard roof.

56 Almshouses are not really public buildings, but people's homes. Often their architecture sets them apart from the run of the mill. That is certainly the case when dealing with Ellison House – the former Windsor Almshouses opened by Queen Victoria herself in 1863. The architect is unknown – which is a pity.

56 A detail of the superb polychrome brickwork of the former Windsor Almshouses.

57 The Theatre Royal on Thames Street is the latest in a long line of theatres in the town. Designed by Sir William Shipley it opened in 1908 and had to be be heavily restored after a fire two years later. There is not a great deal to be said about the architecture.

The elderly poor seem to have been comparatively well treated in Windsor since Elizabethan times, with several different charities being founded to help look after them. The grandest surviving example of such concern is also one of the best of its type and date in the country. The term 'almshouse' is sometimes looked upon as being somehow derogatory to those people living in it – although generally only the most deserving of the poor or elderly were allowed in. Nevertheless, in 1989 when the newly restored Windsor Almshouses on Victoria Street were reopened by the Queen Mother, they were renamed Ellison House, after the Victorian vicar of Windsor, Canon Ellison. This splendid complex of red and yellow brick, stone dressings and steep slate roofs, topped off by a wonderfully

58 Chariotts' Charity was built in the same year as the Windsor Almshouses and in a not dissimilar style. It stands just behind the larger complex and served a basically similar function, paid for by Joseph Chariott.

59 On the north side of the High Street this former bank was built as late as 1910 – despite a neoclassical facade that could have been put up seventy years beforehand. Typically, it is only stone-fronted – the main carcass is of brick.

60 Sir Edwin Lutyens was one of the more famous architects of the first half of the twentieth century. He designed this memorial to George V, at the bottom end of Thames Street, in 1936.

61 The Castle Hotel was built in the early nineteenth century and faced with stucco. The sashes on the upper two floors are probably original – but the cross-mullioned ones on the first floor and the larger ones on the ground floor probably date to the early part of this century. The cast-iron balcony seems original – with a then popular decorative motif often called 'heart and honeysuckle' beneath a 'Vitruvian' scroll.

eccentric timber-framed spirelet, had been opened in 1863 by Queen Victoria.

In 1688, Sir Christopher Wren was ordered to remodel the 'playhouse att Windsor', taking advice on how to do so from the 'french Comoedians', though no traces of this theatre survive. The present theatre, in Thames Street, is the latest in a series of theatres and was built in 1908 after a fire destroyed its predecessor. It was designed by Sir William Shipley and, in turn, was damaged by fire in 1910.

None of the other public buildings in the town call for much attention. The former police station complex in Peascod Street is an Edwardian blurred baroque pile of dull brick and stone decoration but it has at least found a new use – and is far better than its modern successor on Alma Road. The public library was never an architectural masterpiece and was made distinctly worse by its 1960s' face-lift.

Houses

There seem to be very few visible remains of medieval houses in the town. There are, though, several medieval houses within the walls of the castle that give an idea of domestic life in the Middle Ages. The castle was not just a defensive work or a royal palace – within it were the homes of the great and the good and their servants, as well as those of the clerics serving the royal household and the chapels, the knights of the various orders and the hundreds of servants who kept the whole place running. Today, dozens of people still live and work within the castle walls.

The great halls that have always been such a feature of the castle were an important element in medieval domestic life. In most homes of any status, the communal hall was the one room where life was lived – people ate, talked and, initially at least, slept. Later, residents had a little more privacy as separate living quarters developed.

Windsor has few obvious survivals of medieval high-status houses, though Marbeck (incidentally, private) within the Lower Ward of the castle has a substantially intact hall with a fine wind-braced roof, and the Chapter Library was once the communal hall of the vicars, built in the early fifteenth century.

The castle does have important early surviving examples of lower-status housing – the various lodgings built in the Lower Ward for the priest vicars in the Horseshoe Cloister close to the east end of the chapel, and those of the Poor and the Military Knights. Such lodgings may seem small and primitive to modern eyes, but would have been luxurious indeed when they were built, providing well-heated and fairly private accommodation at a time when such a thing was virtually unheard of for the majority of the population. The oldest

63 Tucked away in what is now called Curfew Yard is a detached, late medieval, timber-framed wing or extension originally belonging to a house fronting Thames Street. It has had to be heavily restored.

64 Said to date to 1423, and clearly timber framed despite the rendered facade, this late medieval building on Church Lane is one of the oldest in the town. Inside, the ground floor ceiling beams are exposed, and it would appear that the building was jettied on the street frontage and on the near side wall. The Engine House, dated 1803, was therefore probably built into an existing alleyway between buildings to house the fire engine.

portion is the range of the Military Knights, built around 1360, shortly after the Order of the Garter had been founded. Further west, and nearer to Great Gateway, are the new lodgings provided for in the will of Henry VIII for the Poor Knights, and built in the reign of Mary. The Horseshoe Cloister, an early example of brick-nogged timber-work, was built in about 1480 but was heavily restored by Gilbert Scott in 1871. This is two-storey housing of a slightly higher status than the knights' lodgings on the opposite side of the ward.

18 The Horseshoe Cloister in the Lower Ward of the castle provided good two-storey accommodation for the lesser clergy – the priest vicars – of St George's Chapel. They were more spacious homes than those lodgings provided for the Military Knights on the opposite side of the Ward, and were begun in 1478. This view is taken through the gateway from the Lower Ward.

2 The plaque on 7 Church Street commemorates the warrant to execute Charles I in 1648, by which time this rendered timber-framed building may have stood here for over a century. It was probably modernized, with its framing covered over, after newer houses were built in the street in the later seventeenth century.

66 Another rendered timber frame, 140 Peascod Street, seems not to have been jettied and was probably quite late in the timber-framed tradition of Windsor – perhaps dating to the early seventeenth century and being rendered in the eighteenth. Given its position, it probably contained living quarters on the upper floors with a shop below.

In the town itself the oldest houses that survive are mostly no earlier in date than the sixteenth century, by which time the general layout of a house had become little different than it is today – though without the twentieth-century necessities of the bathroom and WC. The hall had shrunk to the size of a lobby, and there were separate rooms for sitting, dining and sleeping. Houses in Windsor tended to be built individually, despite inadequate space, until the end of the eighteenth century. This can be seen in the diversity of the buildings in the town where houses built centuries apart stand side by side.

67 On the corner of Church Lane and Church Street is this nice lesson in changing architectural tastes. The Church Street front suggests a symmetrical, rendered, five-bay, early Georgian house – but the jetty on the right-hand end is a bit of a giveaway. It is actually a large 'double-pile' (note the two parallel roofs), late medieval, timber-framed house possibly dating to the fifteenth century.

68 Behind the symmetrical brick-faced frontage of Nell Gwynn's House, 5–6 Church Street, are a pair of less fashionable timber-framed rear wings possibly built at the same time in the mid-seventeenth century or perhaps a little beforehand. They back on to St Alban's Street – named after the son of Nell and Charles II.

Up until the end of the eighteenth century, and excepting those houses in the town owned or rented by members of the Court or the Military, most of the houses in the middle of Windsor were lived in by the shop keepers and traders. They literally lived above the shop: their houses were adapted on the ground floor for their businesses. This was a traditional domestic arrangement that has only really died out this century – in Windsor and throughout the rest of the country. More and more people of the middle classes began to move out to the leafier suburbs and the town centres gradually began to get deserted.

One of the important architectural developments of the eighteenth century was that of the high-class terrace, derived from those in fashionable places such as Bath and Edinburgh. This innovation came belatedly to Windsor, simply because there was no call for it in a period when the town suffered from

69 The three-gabled William the Fourth public house on Thames Street has a jettied first floor and is clearly a stuccoed timber-framed building, probably of early seventeenth-century date. It used to be the South Western Hotel.

70 Market Cross House, on the edge of the High Street, is one of those delightful buildings that stay in the memory long after the grander and more predictable ones have been forgotten. This leaning, timber-framed structure is thought to have been built in 1687 and altered in the eighteenth century – which may have been when its structural problems started.

the neglect of the castle. After George III's return, a few such terraces were built, particularly in the early nineteenth century and along King's Road close to the Home Park. In design, these stock-brick rows were very similar to contemporary work in London and the newly fashionable sea-bathing resorts like Brighton or Margate. They have little ornamentation and only a few, like Adelaide Terrace with its central pediment, attempt to emulate the grand, unified, palace front used so effectively elsewhere. The terraced house went 'downmarket' throughout the century as speculators saw it as a cheap way to build housing, and the middle classes looked to other, more individual, forms of building. In Windsor the grand terrace did survive into the mid-Victorian era, seen in a Gothic-detailed terrace totally out of keeping with the rusticity of Mill Lane,

71 Sir Christopher Wren had strong links with Windsor. His father was dean, and his son the local MP. This pedimented two-storey house, on Thames Street close to the bridge, is said to have been designed by Wren as his own home in the late seventeenth century. However, the details all seem to point to a slightly later date, early in the eighteenth century. Could it be that it was his son, another Christopher, who lived here?

72 Elm Place, despite horrible modern extensions on one half of the front to St Leonard's Road, is a pleasant early to mid-eighteenth-century house. Its distinctive feature is this full-height canted bay window, suffering a little from structural defects but all the more picturesque as a result.

73 Hadleigh House on Sheet Street, three storeys high and five bays wide, is one of the finest Georgian houses in Windsor, and is best seen from a little way down Victoria Street. It was probably built in the very last years of the eighteenth century and has fine gate ironwork.

Clewer, for example, and the astonishing neo-Jacobean Queen's Terrace, King's Road, *c.* 1849 designed by Teulon.

The nineteenth century saw the ever-increasing popularity of the great English 'semi' – and early in the century virtually all the houses in the middle-class developments around Clarence Crescent and Holy Trinity Church were of this type. Quite why the semi became so popular is unclear. There was plenty of room to build large detached houses, although buyers wanted their properties to front the street. The houses were built for people with plenty of money, often for military officers or minor courtiers, and had plenty of room in their three floors, attics and basements. Perhaps the idea of approaching a building that looked twice as large as your actual house gave a greater feeling of prosperity. The earlier

74 Stucco – a render lined to resemble stone but later often painted – was in vogue for much of the early nineteenth century. The Limes, on Victoria Street, is of this period. The ground floor stucco is rusticated – being more deeply etched. Notice how it is not quite symmetrical, with larger rooms to the left. The oversized capital of the pilasters are Greek Ionic. It is nice to see a house still with railings.

75 A portion of Brunswick Terrace in King's Road. The name no doubt relates to the much abused wife of George IV – Caroline of Brunswick-Wolfenbuttell. George was forced to marry her in 1795 and this terrace was probably built soon afterwards. He spent most of their marriage trying to divorce the poor woman, and even refused to let her attend his coronation.

76 William IV's queen, Adelaide of Saxe-Coburg, was an altogether happier lady. In Windsor, she seems to have been popular, with her name used several times for buildings. This is the grandest, Adelaide Terrace, built in 1831. It is stuccoed and eighteen bays long – the central four beneath a pediment or attached portico. Strictly speaking, it is architecturally wrong: porticoes should have an odd number of pilasters or columns, and this one has four.

77 York Place, Sheet Street, is a stock-brick terrace probably dating from the second quarter of the nineteenth century and designed by a Robert Tebbott. It has one or two notable features, such as the pilasters and the first-floor band course. These echo the great neoclassical houses of the past, with the tallest floor on the first floor above a low ground floor – or 'rustic'. The terrace may have been named after the Duke of York, son of George III, who died in 1827.

78 Adelaide Square seems to have been an attempt at large-scale development of the type pioneered by John Wood in Bath, and continued by others for much of the Georgian and Regency period. This is the north side of the 'square', which appears never to have been finished. The houses probably date from the 1830s or '40s.

79 Samuel Teulon's eccentric Queen's Terrace in King's Road is a deliberate attempt at historicism, bringing to life the idea of the great Jacobean mansions of the early seventeenth century. Built in 1849, it is a barely restrained riot of brick and stone, prickling with chimneys and shaped gables.

80 This house right by the Windsor end of the bridge on Thames Street would at one time have been in a prime location, its occupants enjoying the views over the busy river from the Regency balcony. It appears to date from the early years of the nineteenth century, towards the end of the Georgian era of brick, symmetrical buildings.

examples clung to some ideas of Georgian elegance and simplicity of proportion, but towards the end of the century decoration had become more and more florid – and generally Gothic. The semi has, of course, survived to the present day and looks like it will continue to be one of the most popular forms of house design.

Grand detached houses continued to be built throughout Victoria's reign, although their grounds got smaller and smaller as the available space was taken up. Some of the end of the century and early Edwardian houses may be rather mechanical in their decorative treatment – and need considerable upkeep – but surely some consideration must be given to their preservation and renovation. In contrast, other houses were more influenced by the Arts and Crafts movement, and possess

81 On the corner of King's Road and Adelaide Square is the curving, stuccoed facade of the Royal Adelaide Hotel, described by the famous architectural historian and critic Nikolaus Pevsner, perhaps unkindly, as being 'fag-end of classical'. Again, the building probably dates from about the 1830s.

82 The late Georgian terrace, 4–6 Park Street, is not really a terrace – there are distinct construction breaks between the brickwork of each house. No. 4 was, at one time, the Black Horse Inn, and has a yard behind; no. 5 is also known as Ann Foorde's House. Behind the parapet, the roofs are of the Mansard type, with a double slope allowing more headroom in the attics. The name is taken from a seventeenth-century French architect called Mansart.

83 Not all terraces, even in the earlier nineteenth century, were grand. Grove Place, probably built in the middle of the century, is a worthy yet unpretentious terrace in Grove Road.

84 The streets around Holy Trinity were laid out in the 1830s and '40s and lined with spacious semi-detached houses with vaguely classical detailing. The overall design has been impinged upon by the unsympathetic buildings of the technical college.

85 In some ways, the Gardner Cottages were influenced by the Prince Consort's examples. Beyond this throughway between the only decorated part of the large quadrangle of two-storey terraces is a huge open space. This is the Arthur Road side, built in 1870.

86 The Prince Consort Cottages off Alexandra Road provided good accommodation for the working classes and stand as a tribute to Prince Albert's concern for the well-being of ordinary people and to the skills of one of the great pioneers of working-class houses, Henry Roberts. The style is simple and elegant – more satisfying than the more decorative prototypes produced by Roberts for the Great Exhibition of 1851.

considerable charm and architectural qualities; in such cases there should be no question of demolition.

Towards the other end of the social scale, living conditions for Windsor's working classes and those in poverty had been poor for centuries. Increased pressure was also put on the limited housing stock when people who had been living, more or less officially, within the castle were cleared out as part of the rebuilding programmes and the houses next to it were demolished at the same time.

Prince Albert, for all his faults, was deeply concerned with the well-being of the poor – and, in particular, with the poor in Windsor. He was the guiding force behind and patron of the worthy, though long-windedly titled, Royal Association for Improving the Condition of Labourers and the Working

87 Lockerbie, in Osborne Road, is a typical late Victorian home of a wealthy businessman or courtier. Its design, reminiscent of a French chateau, is actually quite simple. Another nearby has an identical layout but Tudor details.

88 Frances House on Frances Road is a turn-of-the-century house – large and over-detailed but it still has character.

89 Netley Villa – a typical house in a typical late nineteenth-century terrace – though one more covered than most with terracotta decoration. This range on Alexandra Road was probably built in the 1890s.

90 There is little that can be said in praise of Ward Royal. The flats are spacious and well kept, but the whole complex has a frighteningly inhuman scale and no architectural soul.

91 The good modern architect is still perfectly capable of designing good buildings if the site is right and the money available. This private house is on White Lilies Island in the Thames at Clewer, where there was plenty of space and greenery to balance the harder lines of the building

92 The prestigious terrace continued to survive in Windsor well into the mid-nineteenth century – with several different styles used. This house in Sheet Street has overblown pseudo-neoclassical details that show the final degeneration of the Georgian style.

93 The mid-Victorian neo-Gothic terrace with its busy decoration and decidedly urban character is a little out of place in Mill Lane, Clewer, which otherwise retains its village feel.

Classes at Windsor, Eton, Clewer, Holy Trinity, Old Windsor, Sunningfield, Sunningdale, Windlesham, Dathcet and Egham – generally known, for short, as the Windsor Royal Society, founded in 1849. One of its aims was 'to promote and carry out the improvement of the dwellings of the working classes'. At the Great Exhibition at the Crystal Palace in 1851 the prince had been closely involved in the design of a new type of high-standard working-class housing designed by Henry Roberts – an important landmark in architectural history. Using these as the basic model, the Windsor Royal Society shortly afterwards built two rows of houses on either side of a central green off Alexandra Road. The houses at the Great Exhibition had been given vaguely Jacobean trimmings – these had virtually none but nevertheless managed to be aesthetically pleasing by their human scale and interesting profiles. In their construction, they incorporated iron for beams and some staircases, as well as hollow bricks, all to aid fire protection. These early examples of philanthropic housing continued to be maintained by the original Trust until 1969.

Sadly, most of the builders and developers involved in the huge working-class districts springing up in and around the old town were often less philanthropic. Battalions of buff-brick terraces were not always well built or well sited. There were exceptions. One remarkable quadrangle of fairly humble terraced houses, to the east of Arthur Road, is Gardner Cottages, dated to 1870 – a time when Clewer Fields were being developed. There was room to build quite intensively on the site, but instead a large grassed square exists within the block of houses – enough for at least two other streets if the greed had been there. The space comes as something of a surprise to anyone venturing through the only decorated portion of these otherwise quite plain two-storey houses.

The houses of Windsor in the twentieth century have developed in more or less the same way as any other town of similar size in the south-east. The town has some good examples of interwar housing, for example in Bolton Road, and some not so good examples. The royal influence is still felt, especially with the continuing tradition of providing good quality accommodation for the workers of the parks. Only since the 1960s have the flat and the maisonette become a part of Windsor's housing scene – and it surely can be done a lot better than Ward Royal.

Industrial
Buildings

According to an 1840 gazetteer, Windsor 'has neither any particular branch of manufacture nor any trade, except what is necessary for the supply of the inhabitants'. Indeed, it has never been an important industrial town, but does, nevertheless, possess some industrial buildings of interest, mainly connected with transport. Virtually nothing survives of its once important trade on the river, and today it is the preserve of pleasure craft of all shapes and sizes – from rowing boats to floating gin palaces that look ready to cross the Atlantic but which probably seldom venture further downstream than Teddington Lock.

The river provided a hindrance to road traffic, of course, and there was a bridge linking Windsor with Eton as early as the twelfth century – if not before. The present bridge is a lot younger. Its foundation stone was laid in July 1822 by the Duke of York, and the bridge was designed by Charles Hollis. The contractor was a William Moore, who died during the work, and it was completed by his son, Richard Moore, and officially opened on 1 June 1824. Over 200 ft in length, its three arches are of cast iron, rising from granite abutments and piers. Originally it was a toll bridge, the money being used to repay the loan and interest of the building costs. The tolls were finally removed at the end of the nineteenth century. A new bypass upstream crosses the river on a new and less distinguished bridge, and the old bridge is now restricted to pedestrian traffic.

The arrival of the railway at Windsor was delayed by vested

94 Windsor Bridge, now, thankfully, closed to road traffic, links the town with Eton, and Berkshire with Buckinghamshire. There has been a bridge here for centuries, but this one with its three cast-iron arches was opened in 1824 and was designed by Charles Hollis.

95 Isambard Kingdom Brunel built this 'bow-string' bridge across the river to carry a branch line of the Great Western Railway in 1849. It has a span of over 202 ft – very adventurous for those days.

96 Sir William Tite designed the London & South Western Railway's Riverside station, dated 1851 but opened a little before. The tall openings on the right allowed cavalry easy access to the trains.

97 Well away from her subjects, Queen Victoria could wait for her trains in a purpose-built royal waiting-room by the Riverside station, also designed by Tite.

98 Not to be outdone, the Great Western company also provided a private royal waiting-room at their station nearer to the centre of the town. To appear even-handed, the queen used the services of both companies. Recently, this was the home of the Royalty & Empire Exhibition, which closed down in 1993.

98 The Great Western's terminus was largely rebuilt at the end of the nineteenth century. The entrance off Thames Street is a memorable one.

interests in both the borough and across the river in Eton – being particularly opposed by the college. The Great Western Railway's main London to Bristol line passed through Slough just to the north in 1838 but no station was allowed there until 1840 and another ten years elapsed before a short branch was built from there to Windsor. The line had to be carried above the often flooded river meadows on the approach to the town on a rather ugly, brick viaduct, but the bridge over the river is a little special. Designed by the renowned engineer of the Great Western, Isambard Kingdom Brunel, it is a wrought-iron 'bow-string' construction with a single span of 202 ft between the brick abutments. Finished in 1849, in many ways it was an experimental forerunner of Brunel's great Saltash bridge linking Devon and Cornwall.

The terminus of the branch line meant the destruction of notorious slums at the back of George Street. That first station was rebuilt at the end of the nineteenth century, much of the brick and stone structure dating from 1897; the private waiting-room and platform used by Queen Victoria still stands and has been restored.

From the opposite direction, the London and South Western Railway built a branch line to a station not far from the bridge. They called it Windsor & Eton. The station buildings were designed by Sir William Tite, who designed many stations throughout Britain. This one, a brick Gothic design, had, like its Great Western counterpart, a separate waiting-room complex for Queen Victoria, which also survives. The station building has a good wrought-iron canopy and its side wall is pierced by tall arches designed to allow the cavalry easy access to the trains. The design's main flaw is the very amateurish use of black-glazed bricks to outline dates and ciphers on the walls facing the castle.

The Great Park

The Saxon kings loved hunting in the area around Old Windsor; the Norman kings made it their own. From then on, the royal prerogative to hunt in what became the Great Park was jealously guarded and anyone doing so without permission was subject to harsh punishment – even death. One of the main reasons that this area was good for hunting is that it was good for little else. William Cobbett, on one of his *Rural Rides* in 1822 noted that 'A very large part of the Park is covered with heath or rushes, sure sign of execrable soil' – and thus was no good for agriculture.

The park's boundaries have fluctuated over the centuries and at their greatest extent stretched almost as far as Reading to the west. Now the Great Park is much smaller and since the end of the seventeenth century has been used for more peaceful recreations – and has become more accessible to the subjects.

The park, now divided into the Home and Great Parks, is not really a part of the town but has always been a royal playground – and is dotted with buildings that reflect this. These include not only the houses and lodges used by royalty and their guests, but also buildings used by the large community of people needed to keep the estate going and a selection of architectural follies and monuments. By no means all of these buildings are generally accessible, or even visible, to the public, and it should be stressed that while much of the Great Park is open to the public, little of the

100 The Crown have always provided accommodation for the workers of the castle and the parks. Often these were used as excuses for architectural fancy – such as this set of cottages designed by Samuel Teulon in 1853. These are on the King's Road, just outside the Queen Anne's Gate.

100 A detail of a second set of houses of the same date, on the opposite side of the road. The brick bond is unusual, with courses of bricks laid on their sides instead of their bottoms – sometimes called a 'rat-trap' bond. This meant that fewer bricks were needed, although the bond would not be as strong as conventional ones.

101 Queen Anne's Gate marks the end of the King's Road and the beginning of the Great Park. The late seventeenth-century brick house was remodelled in the 1830s in a cottage *ornée* style and bears the initials of William IV.

102 At first sight this pair of mid-twentieth-century semis on the King's Road close to Teulon's cottages of 1853 do not seem very interesting at all. A closer look reveals that they are dated 1936 – and the figures E VIII R appear with the date. Edward VIII reigned for most of 1936 before being forced to abdicate in December because of his love for the American divorcee, Mrs Simpson. These simple cottages are one of the few architectural reminders of his reign.

103 The Royal Mausoleum in the Home Park may seem to us a morbid monument to put in what was effectively the castle's garden – but the Victorians certainly had a fascination with death. It cost the then fabulous sum of £200,000 and took nearly ten years to build – it was finished in 1871. The architects were A. J. Humbert and a Professor Gruner of Germany. It is seldom open to the public. This postcard, incidentally, dates back to the early years of this century.

Home Park is – and most of the buildings within each are either only opened on rare occasions or not at all; generally they are very much out of bounds. The parks have their own distinct character and their architectural delights – but these are really outside the scope of this book. Nevertheless, a walk up to the Copper Horse at the top of the Long Walk is to be recommended; from there, the view down to the castle and the town that grew up in its shadow is one of the best in Britain.

Index

Page numbers in bold indicate illustrations